Welcome

Welcome to your *My Little Ogichidaa: An Indigenous Lullaby* lesson plans.

Here, you will find multiple lesson plans for you to use within your classroom to further explore the content in this book. This includes comprehension questions, word searches, and some creative projects.

All of these lesson plans have been approved by the author, Willie Poll.

Medicine Wheel Publishing acknowledges that this lesson plan was created on the unceded traditional territory of the Coast Salish People including the Sc'ianew people, the Lekwungen people and the T'Sou-ke people.

Contents

Willie Poll

My Little Ogichidaa: An Indigenous Lullaby Lesson Plan

April 16th, 2024
ISBN: 978-1-77854-0332

$7.99 CAD / $5.95 USD
ISBN 978-1-77854-033-2
50595>
9 781778 540332

Introduction

Before Reading Activities

Introduce the title of the book to your class, and lead a discussion about the title.

- What do you think the word *Ogichidaa* could mean?
- Read aloud the subtitle, *An Indigenous Lullaby*. How might language be used in this book? Who might the narrator in the book be speaking to?
- Think of any lullabies you may know of. What are these lullabies about? What style of language is used?

Next, move on to discussing the illustrations on the cover, to find more clues as to what the book may be about.

- Who is pictured on the cover? Is there anything noticeable about this person? How is she holding her soon-to-be-born child?
- What else can you see on the cover? Are there any patterns you notice? What might that mean for the story?

Take some time to look at the back of the cover and read the description. Together, make note of any keywords you notice. Also note any questions that may come up after reading this description to return to once you have finished the book.

- Were your predictions on what *Ogichidaa* meant correct? Now knowing that this word means *Warrior* in Anishinaabemowin, what might this tell us about the book?

Read both the author and illustrator bios at the end of the book.

- Do the creators speak to any inspirations or influences that contribute to their work? How may that influence the story, as well as the artwork?
- Note down which traditional territory each creator is from. Mark each of these on a map of Turtle Island.

Activity 1

Comprehension Questions

Read the book, *My Little Ogichidaa*, with your class. Ensure that you take some time to go over the letter from the author, Willie, and each dedication.

When you are ready, give students some comprehension questions to help consolidate their learning. If they are stuck on a question, they can refer back to the book for help. Note that some of the answers may be found in the letter from Willie or the dedications.

- What does the word *Ogichidaa* mean, and what language is it written in?
- Who did the author, Willie, dedicate this book to?
- Who is the parent in the book speaking to?
- How do you think the parent feels towards her soon-to-be-born child? Why do you think that?
- What do the pins on pages 21–22 represent? Why do you think the people on these pages are wearing red? Look to Willie's dedication if you are unsure.
- On page 15, the parent speaks about her child being related to the water, the plants, and the animals. How does this worldview help us to grow in how we relate to the world around us?
- What do you think it means when the parent says, "you will break cycles/ Your love will spread for miles and miles"? What cycles do you think she is referring to?
- Using rhyme, write several hopes and wishes you would want to pass on to a little Ogichidaa in your life. This could be your younger sibling, a cousin, or another friend or family member.
- Look at the artwork in the book. Notice how the illustrator, Hawlii, connects different elements together through vines, plants, umbilical cords, and so on. Pick one example and write about why you think Hawlii did this.

Activity 1 *Continued*

- Notice how there is a section at the beginning of the book to write a letter to a little Ogichidaa in your life. On a separate sheet of paper, create your own letter, starting with "Little Ogichidaa, my wish for you…" This letter could even be addressed to a younger version of yourself, or your wishes for your future self.

- Which part of the book is your favourite? Write about what happens during this part, and why you think it is your favourite. Mention the artwork, as well as the story.

- Why do you think the parent says, "take up your space/Because you and our people belong in this place"? Why is this important to acknowledge?

Come together as a class to have a discussion about the important messages within this book.

- Why do you think Willie refers to the soon-to-be-born child as a Warrior? Acknowledge the realities Indigenous children have to face that others may not. Look to Willie's letter for help.

- Acknowledge the important work that is being done by Indigenous groups to create change and a space for healing across Turtle Island. This includes the work of the Moosehide Campaign and the Orange Shirt Society with the Orange Shirt Day: Every Child Matters movement. Refer to pages 21–22 and pages 11–12, and note all the ways both Willie and Hawlii acknowledge these important, Indigenous-led movements.

- Notice how Willie frequently honours and acknowledges the role our ancestors have in who we become. Go through the book and make note of how many times ancestors are acknowledged, both in writing and the artwork. Guide a discussion with your class about the ancestors of the land and the territory that you are currently residing on, and why it is important to honour them.

- One of the important messages in this book is about celebrating and speaking to the immense power of Indigenous love. Discuss with your class all the ways Willie honours the power and beauty of Indigenous love throughout the book. Why is this important to speak about?

Activity 2

Word Art Activities

This activity will require using words from the book to complete a creative activity. Words, phrases, or sentences can be chosen by either the student or the teacher. Students will print in tiny letters to create the finished detail on their artwork.

Two activities have been included for you to choose from, to use with your class. For each of these, partial images have been included to be a starting point, with lines to be completed with sentences from the book. Provided are a range of adaptations, depending on how complex you would like the activity to be for your students. The templates for each activity will go underneath the chosen worksheet. Bold, dark lines will show through white paper. If more light is needed, have students put the patterns on a window.

Mother Word Art Activity

Please see the following three options for adaptations of this activity. The main template, which is used for all adaptations, can be found on page 10. This will go under the worksheet to be completed. It is recommended to print the template and worksheets onto 8.5 x 11 inch pages.

Option One

This project requires the most amount of detail to be added. For this activity, you will have to add the mother's legs, the vine, and your own words from the book. Please see the Option One worksheet on page 8 for students to complete. Please also see the finished sample for how this would look.

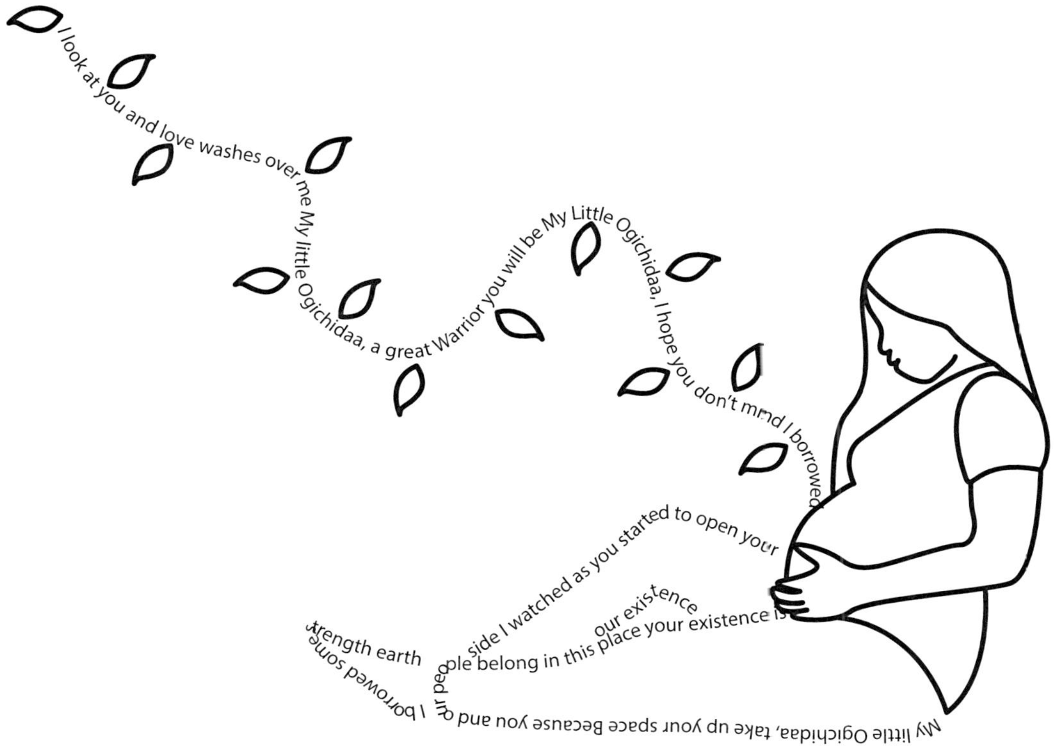

Sample for Mother Word Art Activity, Option One

Option Two

For this activity, a moderate amount of detail is needed. You will only have to add the mother's legs and the vine. You could either use the words provided on the worksheet to complete the image, or complete it with drawn lines. Please see the Option Two worksheet on page 9.

Option Three

This activity requires the least amount of detail to be added. You just have to add the vine to the artwork. See the Option Three worksheet on page 10. You could either use the words provided to complete the image, or complete it with drawn lines.

Option One: Mother Word Art Activity Worksheet

You bring hope to all our
relations that live on this earth

You bring hope to all our
relations that live on this earth

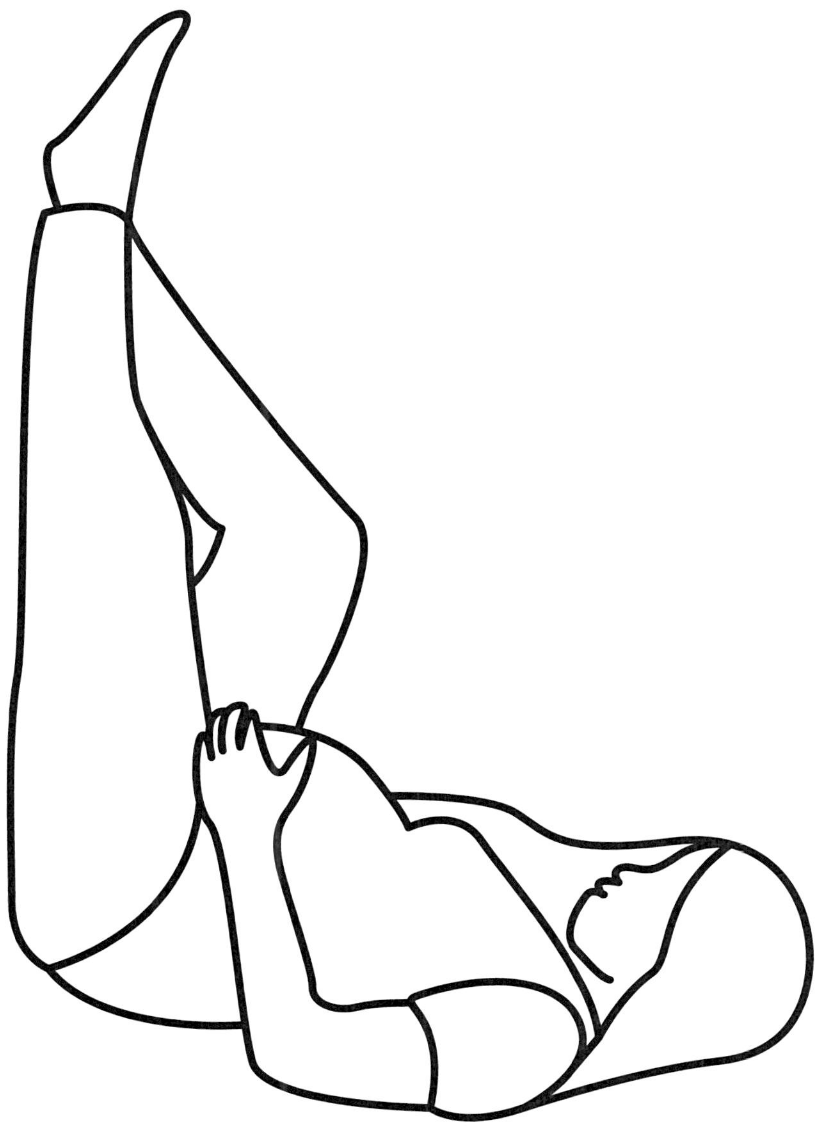

Feather Word Art Activity

For this activity, students have two options. Students can trace on the lines of the feather to finish an art project with lines, or they can use words from the book to finish the detail on the feather.

The lines for the feather will show through onto the worksheet once the feather template (found on page 13) is placed under a copy of the worksheet (found on page 12). It is recommended to print these onto 8.5 x 11 inch pages.

The blank lines provided on the worksheet could be used for writing lines from the book. You could also adapt this activity to have the students give a response to the book on those blank lines.

Please see the following sample with traced lines added to the feather to see an option of how this could be completed.

Sample of Feather Word Art Activity, Option One

Activity 2 Feather Activity Worksheet

Activity 2 Feather Activity Template

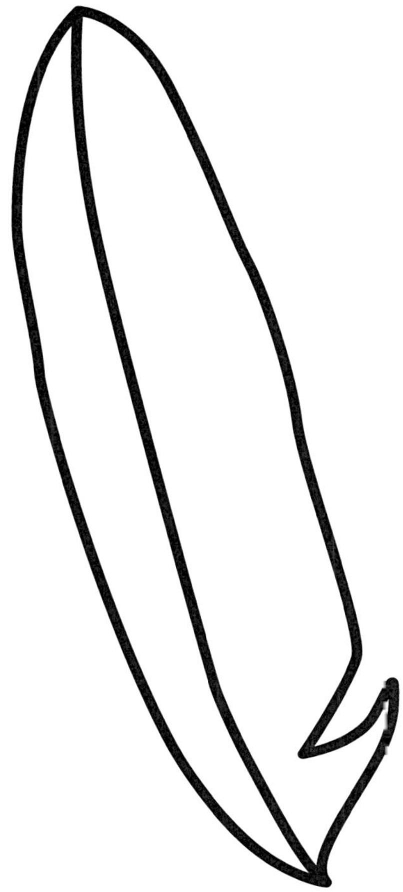

Activity 3

Growing Expectations for our Little Warriors

The imagery of the growing vine in Willie's book speaks to growth. This creative activity will get students thinking about what they can become by setting goals for themselves. Everyone, teachers and students alike, may also be challenged to think about the many opportunities we can bring to light for little warriors.

First, have students think and share about what they remember from being a baby. Have them share their own memories of growing up, what they have been told by others about their early years, or any pictures they have from that time.

After stories have been shared, focus the discussion on all the great things in the book that the mother wishes upon her soon-to-be-born Ogichidaa. Have students brainstorm ideas of what actions they could take, or traits they could embody, to become a warrior.

From the list that was created, have students print one idea onto a paper leaf. The leaf template on the following page could be used, or students could create their own leaves! Repeat this by writing other aspirations onto separate leaves. Next, on a bulletin board, attach the leaves to a growing vine that can be made from either construction paper or green rope. Please see the examples on the right.

This activity serves as a reminder that warriors come in all sizes and ages!

Activity 3 Growing Expectations Leaf Template

Activity 4

Wordsearch for Younger Students

My Little Ogichidaa

L	Y	K	G	H	O	D	A	N	C	E	A
N	R	P	R	O	T	E	C	T	F	G	L
M	O	U	N	T	A	I	N	S	B	V	O
G	R	O	W	K	M	O	V	E	L	W	V
N	X	P	H	O	P	E	D	H	O	Y	E
P	L	O	V	F	S	Q	X	F	O	I	Q
Z	I	W	A	R	R	I	O	R	M	F	P
K	V	C	T	R	U	T	H	R	Q	G	P

Find the following words in the puzzle.
Words are hidden → and ↓

MOUNTAINS
PROTECT
WARRIOR
BLOOM

DANCE
TRUTH
GROW
HOPE

LOVE
MOVE

Activity 5

Wordsearch for Older Students

My Little Warrior

J C R C Q B M K K B O R R O W E D T

I D O R U R U K N H W I L D L Y D W

C R O L E D F A X O E G X K G X I A

U L E G O L R E N S W A N T V T S S

L A H J I N A E T C P L R D F W R H

T N V H O C I T A I E I E T H C U E

U G X T B I H Z I M N S R D G Q P S

R U C O V S C I A O E I T I G U T P

E A B T K M T E D T N R E O T E I D

T G C X K V X A N A I S X S R S O Y

M E D I C I N E U X A O J C T S N Q

A K H A A N I M A L S M N B L L J A

Find the following words in the puzzle.
Words are hidden → ↓ and ↘

COLONIZATION
DISRUPTION
OGICHIDAA
ANCESTORS
RELATIONS
KNOWLEDGE
BORROWED
LANGUAGE
MEDICINE
SPIRITS
REJOICE
TINIEST
DREAMER
ANIMALS
CULTURE
WILDLY
WASHES
HEART

Activity 6

Colouring Pages

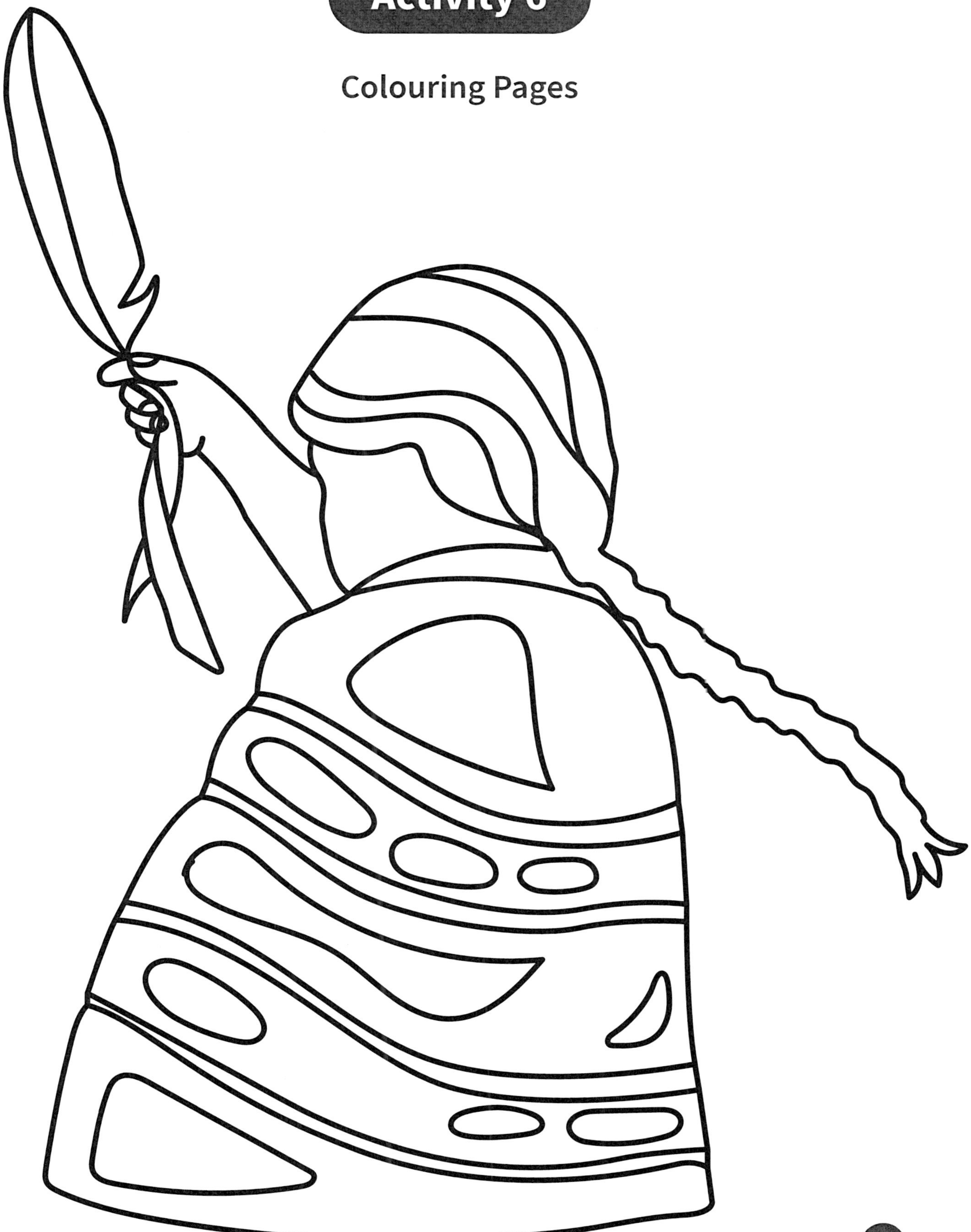

Activity 6 Colouring Page Two

Activity 6 Colouring Page Three

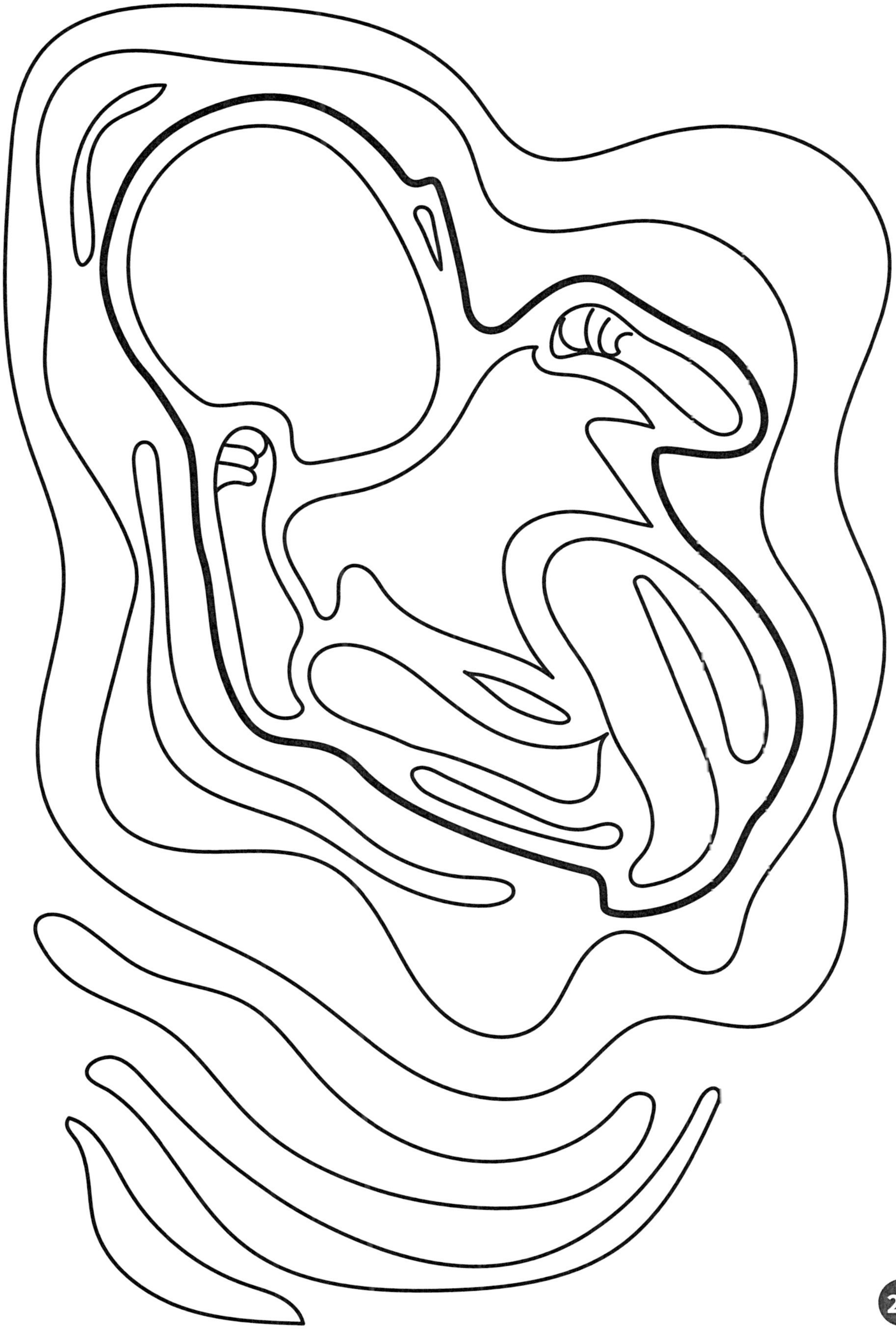